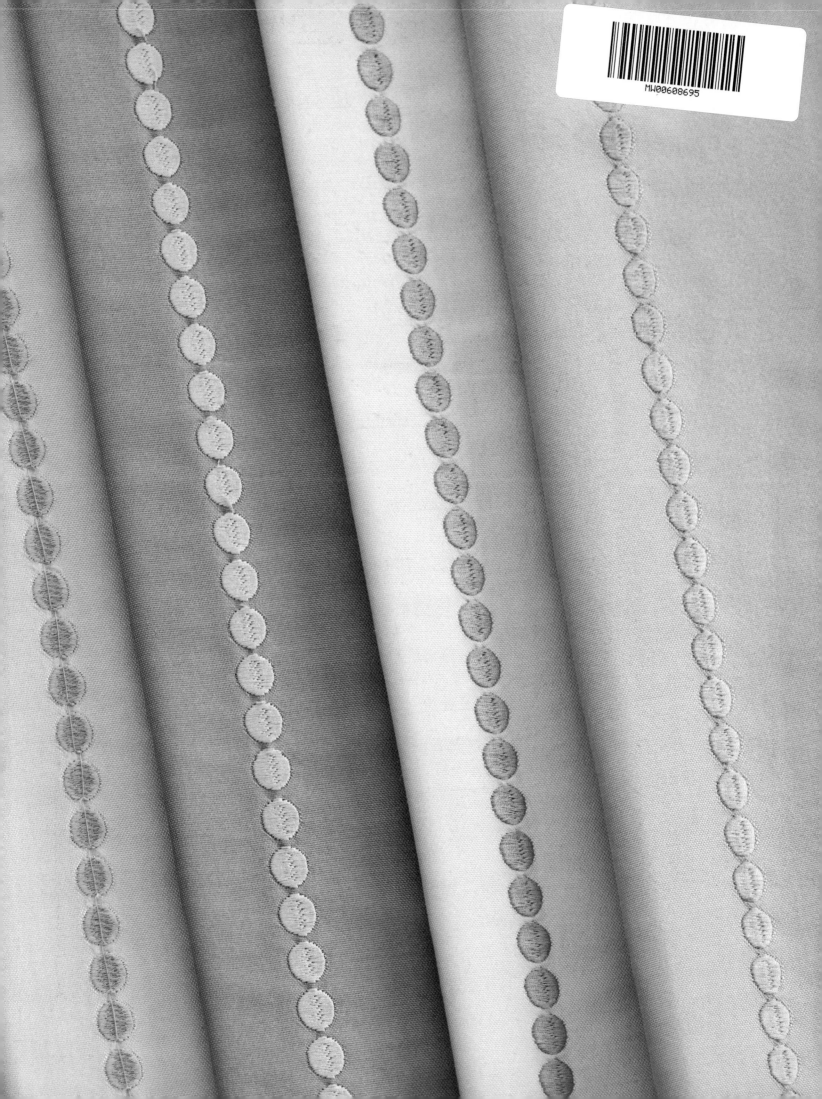

THROUGH A DESIGNER'S EYE
A FOCUS ON INTERIORS

THROUGH A DESIGNER'S EYE

A FOCUS ON INTERIORS

MATTHEW PATRICK SMYTH

FOREWORD BY WENDY GOODMAN
WRITTEN WITH JUDITH NASATIR

THE MONACELLI PRESS

For Jean Vallier for thirty-eight years of being there.

For the memory of artists Robert Courtright and Bruno Romeda, whose work flows through many of my projects and whose friendship is much missed.

For the late Dietrich Weismann, who, along with Philippa, gave me the confidence to quit my safe, comfortable job on the day after Black Monday, October 19, 1987. Dick said it was the most perfect time to start my own firm. It was. Philippa said we would have many great adventures. And we still do!

Finally, for Gloria Vanderbilt. I will always be grateful to Wendy Goodman for introducing us.

CONTENTS

My portrait of Wendy.

FOREWORD

Matthew Patrick Smyth has always reminded me of a character in a Willa Cather novel with his straightforward kindness, generosity, and impeccable manners. The first time I met him was at a cocktail party hosted by the gregarious, slightly witchy, photographer and antiques dealer, Roger Prigent. Roger's fabulous penthouse living room was filled with all sorts of fabulous New York characters bubbling over with shared gossip; I noticed Matthew taking it all in off to one side of the room. I wanted to meet this person, and Roger led me over for an introduction. That was the beginning of a friendship where we have shared our longest, deepest conversations and laughter in his car as he has driven us to so many wonderful places, most notably over the years to the very different country houses that he has shared with his husband, the French writer Jean Vallier.

During these drives, a clear picture of Matthew's character came into focus, as he described his childhood and I gleaned what it meant being eldest of five siblings. His father worked on Wall Street by day, and on and off weekends as manager of the Copacabana nightclub, while his mother took care of the family at home. The early death of his father meant that his mother went back to school and trained to become a nurse to support the family, while Matthew at seventeen shouldered the responsibilities of being the eldest. The twists and turns of Matthew's life leading up to his stellar career as an interior designer, and less well-known but equally magnificent talent as a photographer, were shaped by many things including bicycle rides as a kid in his native Washington Heights neighborhood, exploring everything from the Cloisters to the art deco architecture of the Grand Concourse. Matthew imagined a life in the theater before his practical side took him to a business school. Then, after myriad interim jobs, his portfolio of photographs earned him a place at the Fashion Institute of Technology studying interior design. The rest is history. Matthew's work is as varied as his clients' tastes, but the one thing that remains consistent is his brilliance at delivering authentic beauty and true comfort no matter where his talent lands.

—Wendy Goodman

INTRODUCTION

The eye constantly evolves. The more we look, the more we experience, the better we are able to see. This is why I travel as much as I do. And why I love the created worlds of the movies, the theater, and the opera. I am constantly searching for that special design something—a handcrafted detail, an insight into history, a sense of surroundings, a moment of drama, a particular atmosphere—that sparks a fresh way of thinking about how to put together a room or home for the those who will live in it. Rediscovering photography in this age of the phone camera has brought home the truth of the many different ways we see. I have found that peering through a lens with a fixed field of vision affects not only my decisions about what and how to shoot, but also how I weed through and edit the pictures I take. Like the design process, the sorting of pictures involves my critical, analytical, and emotional judgement. What I have also found is that it translates, directly and indirectly, into the way I work as a designer.

Taking pictures again has made me rethink just about everything I have learned about interiors over the years. It has also shown me that even as tastes and styles change, as they inevitably do, my own included, what captures my eye has remained remarkably consistent. As a photographer, I love the same things I do as an interior designer: scale, composition, line, color, texture, and, above all, balance. Surprisingly, I can trace the arc of the pictures I today take back to the elevations I have drawn since my student days at the Fashion Institute of Technology.

Elegant and whimsical, this Regency mirror encapsulates
so much of what I love about design from that period.

It was Gloria Vanderbilt who inspired me to return to photography. Collaborating with her for the first time at the Kips Bay Decorator Show House in 2009 on the re-creation of the bedroom her aunt Gertrude Vanderbilt Whitney decorated for her as a teenager made me look at everything a little bit differently. Gloria's work, whether painting, sculpture, or collage, always celebrated the most extreme details. From the start, I was especially taken with her use of collage. But even in her other artwork, she honored the tiniest elements, including all sorts of bits and things she found at flea markets or even on the street. As I got to know her, I found her ability to see the beauty in the smallest things and her joy in putting these pieces together to create something so much more powerful both inspiring and eye-opening. When we collaborated again, in 2014 on the salon space for her exhibition "The Left Hand Is the Dreamer," I remember returning to my office building, one of Ely Jacques Kahn's elegant art deco skyscrapers, and noticing its suave architectural ornament again as if it were in high definition. By then, I think I had been walking through its embellished doors for five years. Early on, I was so delighted by Kahn's disciplined eye for detail and the flourishes he created with pattern and texture. But with everyday familiarity, these elements had receded into the background. Knowing Gloria was a wake-up call, a reminder to always look closely at my surroundings and not take any part of them for granted. And she, along with the emergence of the phone camera, led me back to photography.

From the first time I picked up a camera as a seventeen-year-old, I was excited by the way that it pushed me to look at details, to tighten my field of vision on the moment right in front of me. The camera made me see differently and think harder. When I came back to it, I was a little rusty. But I found I had really missed looking through the lens.

The process of design for me has always been about seeing the big picture first, working my way in to the smallest elements, then widening my view again. I start every project with the overall floor plan and concept. Then I narrow it down, fine-tuning as I go, space by space, to the last detail, only to build up the interior again in the installation, layer by layer, to the finishing touches of art and the very last pillow. I find I do that with a camera, too, although not quite in the same way. The frame focuses my concentration on the detail, rather than the entire situation. With every photograph I take, I am aware that most people who will see it will picture their own scene from the detail in my image. This is part of the subconscious process that is inherent in the relationship between the photographer and the viewer. What I want that photograph to explore, though, is the why of the beauty. And so I try to home in on one or a few of the most essential and interesting aspects that build that larger picture, that convey the mood or atmosphere of that specific moment. What makes the interior of a particular building different from any other interior? Is it the tracery of the ironwork? Or the profile of the crown molding? Why is one sunset more interesting than another? Is it the way the light hits the tree? Or the shape of the shadow? Because I want my photographs to answer those kinds of questions, I usually aim straight for the detail.

I discovered the joy of taking pictures my senior year in high school. While I had basic lessons in the technical aspects of the camera and darkroom, I really learned by trial and error. I was also lucky enough to have had a good art teacher. He got us to question the why of our choices, to think twice about what we had done so that we could weed out anything mediocre or unnecessary. I can still hear him telling us to ask ourselves, Who cares? That year, I ended up shooting the entire yearbook by myself. Before I graduated, when I still thought I might become a photographer, there was an exhibition in Goshen of my shots of architectural details—the church steeples, crown moldings, columns, and so on, of my hometown (and William Henry Seward's), Florida, New York. The built fabric of the village, which predates the Revolutionary War, is something of a time line of American architecture. Its historic structures include Orange County's second-earliest Presbyterian Church, established in 1741, as well as interesting houses, and commercial and industrial buildings from the eighteenth and nineteenth centuries. Spending my formative years there—we moved from New York City when I was thirteen—sharpened my eye to history and design.

I love the editing process. My high school art teacher's method has stuck with me over the years, although I have adapted it: "Beautiful room, but who cares?" Or "Lovely photograph, but who cares?" "Who cares?" works as both a prod and a restraint. It pushes me to be critical about the purpose of what I am doing—to think hard and long about the meaning and consequences of each choice—and it pulls me back should I be tempted to make selections just for effect. Rooms should have a point of view, an interest, a reason for being. The elements of each interior should be personal and truly specific to the people whose home I am designing. It is important to me that whatever is in their rooms triggers the realization that the rooms are about them. And so I prefer that the furnishings, fabrics, objects, and art all have meaning. When they do, they embody stories and capture moments—just like photographs do, but differently. In the end, I want the people I work with to feel comfortable in their own homes, to live with what they love, to be attached to every element and object, to enjoy every last detail.

The photographer Jay Maisel once said, "Always shoot it now. It won't be the same when you go back." This is so true. From the beginning, my intention with the images I post on social media has been to shape moments. When I have not quite captured the picture I wanted on camera, I will tweak the image in ways that bring the moment back to what I thought it was when I saw it. This way of looking and the process of adjusting has further heightened and deepened my awareness of my surroundings, and the way I experience them. The photographic moments not only document a way of seeing, but they also translate, directly or indirectly, into my design approach. So much of what I do as an interior designer—and so much of what I see as a photographer—is ultimately about line, form, and silhouette. But it is also about finding ways to memorialize transformation and change. The eye constantly evolves. So do we.

A jacquard-woven cotton sateen designed by Lauren Kidwell for Pollack/Weitzner balances the refined against the more rustic sisal floorcovering. Nailhead details and brass accessories add understated touches of brightness.

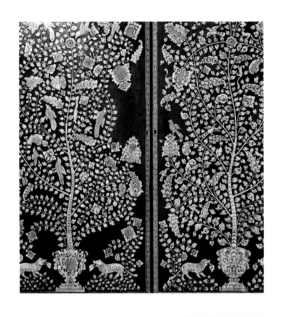

THE HAND

W

e all admire beautiful objects, whether made by hand or produced by machine. But what the hand crafts is one of a kind—the unique result of an individual imagination, a particular set of skills, and an aesthetic intention. Even when the piece is a multiple, a part of a set, it still varies to a degree from its mates because the hand, no matter how gifted and practiced, is never flawless. Similar is not the same. There is a perfect imperfect. And for me, the touch of the hand is a major factor in what transforms a design project into a truly crafted room. There is a place for the manufactured, of course. But if the option and the resources exist for custom work, why compromise?

The ability to commission pieces for a specific space and client adds so many layers to the living space. Craftspeople introduce something indefinable to the pieces they make: the singular touch. Together, we can tweak and twist the piece into a greater degree of specialness while it is in production. The outcome of the original thought is no longer predetermined, and the experience for the client becomes so much more personal. There is nothing quite like the moment when clients grasp the idea of infinite possibility and feel the excitement of having something designed and made just for them.

With seating, there is no such thing as one size fits all. The human body is endlessly variable. Each of us has our own way of sitting and stretching out. Working with an upholsterer, it is possible to adjust chairs and sofas to create that ideal level of comfort: changing the fill in a back and the firmness of a seat to suit; adapting the depth of a seat to fit height

The architect Maurice Fatio incorporated bricks from the Royal Poinciana Hotel, razed during the Depression, into this Palm Beach house, which he designed for the Huntington family. This hand-forged sconce is one of a pair that was in the house when my clients purchased it.

and leg length; modifying the pitch to respond to a personal preference for climbing into and out; making sure a sofa is long enough and sufficiently cushy for naps. All these internal structural elements come into play. So do the externals, such as fabric, details, and trim. As we adjust each of the many factors that go into every piece of upholstery, we are transforming a floor sample from a standard model into something one of a kind.

I often modify or adapt furniture to fit a particular client's lifestyle by turning over elements of the design to a craftsperson to embellish or simplify, to modernize or tweak. Sometimes, we just want to make it function more seamlessly. Suppose we find a great brass table base in Germany, but the glass top that comes with it is not right for the room where we plan to use it. One option might be to have a carpenter prepare a piece of wood, which we would then have lacquered to just the right shade and finish. Another might be to select the perfect piece of stone, and have it shaped and finished to specification. Unless the original piece is from an important maker, it makes sense to change it as necessary. And when it is right, we know it right away.

The great drapery workers are artists as well as craftspeople. They often come in with muslin so we can mock up ideas to imagine how the curtains will look. We might use the same hardware in different locations. But because windows are endlessly varied in shape, style, and dimension, there are no stock solutions for shades and curtains, much less valances, rods, tiebacks, and trim. Every element of the window dressing has to be made to fit the window's dimensions, and to harmonize with the other features of the room.

Whatever the unique solution happens to be, it comes with a set of complications. Today's technology and the global economy have expanded our horizons and access to skilled craftspeople around the world when we cannot find them at home. Over the last decade, I have been working with embroiderers in India, which has such a long and glorious tradition of exquisite handwork. First I went to Mumbai to meet them. Now we communicate via FedEx and Skype.

It may be a cliché to say that being open to the world brings the world and its history home to you, but that does not make it any less true. Recently I worked with some craftspeople in Ireland to create wallpaper for an interior here in New York. We based the pattern on a document damask from a historic house, and custom colored it after checking the palette in the light in both places. Some of the legendary French fabric houses have comparable treasures in their archives, a universe of design beyond what is in their showrooms. It is possible to visit these archives, sort through the document patterns and the plates, and collaborate on something original. The challenge is always time. In our era of immediacy, what so often determines the level of craftsmanship in a project is a willingness to wait.

One client decided to have all her stemware handblown in Venice. We went to Murano to select four different goblets in four colors for her table. Each has a different shape, top, and stem. The colors blend, but they do not match. And none of the goblets lines up exactly with the others. But she loves the handmade. She loves the idea that she has commissioned great artisans to put their skills to work to create pieces just for her. The Venetians have been making glassware for centuries. We are fortunate and grateful to be able to make use of their rich tradition of artistry today.

The craft tradition is the human tradition. Craftspeople and artisans have passed their skills, their trade secrets, and their studios from one generation to the next, from master to apprentice, from parent to child. The knowledge stays in the family when there are interested heirs. If not, the master makes other arrangements, often with a longtime worker, and the cycle continues.

There are many ways to frame the history of interior design and the decorative arts. One common thread is the relationship between benefactors and artisans. Commissioning craftspeople to ply their skills to create the elements of an interior is a minor way of being a patron. Why should that stop? When we invest in artisans and craftspeople, we are investing in history—and in the future.

The veranda, which connects the living room to the dining room and kitchen, has a wall of glass that overlooks the intercoastal waterway. The églomisé mirror, original to the house, first hung in Mrs. Huntington's dressing room. We reframed it and repositioned it here. Covered in handwoven mats from Borneo, the square ottomans add an interesting element of pattern.

The lines and curves of this vignette from the dining room of the Palm Beach house seem to speak eloquently to the details of the monkeys playing cards depicted on the églomisé mirror that commands such attention—and amusement—on the veranda.

NEW TRADITIONS

Most of us are obsessed with what is modern. And most young couples want to live with new things. Choosing to keep heirlooms front and center does not by definition make anyone—or any home—old-fashioned. This young couple, for example, is anything but. They appreciate fine furniture because both of them grew up with it. With two children on the verge of their tween and teen years, the couple planned to renovate their existing apartment to meet their evolving needs. Then they saw this duplex. It was in estate condition, so we reworked every last inch to create the kind of living spaces they wanted: stylish, but not aggressively so, and with favorite pieces handed down from parents and grandparents.

It was clear from day one that the entry was a make-or-break situation because it would set the tone for the entire place. The architect Charlotte Worthy helped us resolve the ungainly space by removing some awkward closets under the stairs, cleaning up the stair line, and reconfiguring the entrance hall with a new coat closet area and powder room.

The living room, which opens off one side of the entry hall, was inspired by a Bernard Buffet painting that belonged to the wife's father, a piece she particularly adored growing up, which now hangs over the fireplace. We incorporated many different periods as well as various pieces handed down from two generations, including a beautiful sofa from her mother that we reupholstered. For chairs to go with it, we

When we began our redesign of this Park Avenue duplex, we knew the entry hall would set the stage for the rest of the apartment. The architect Charlotte Worthy helped us bring the narrow space into sharp focus by developing the sweep of the stairway.

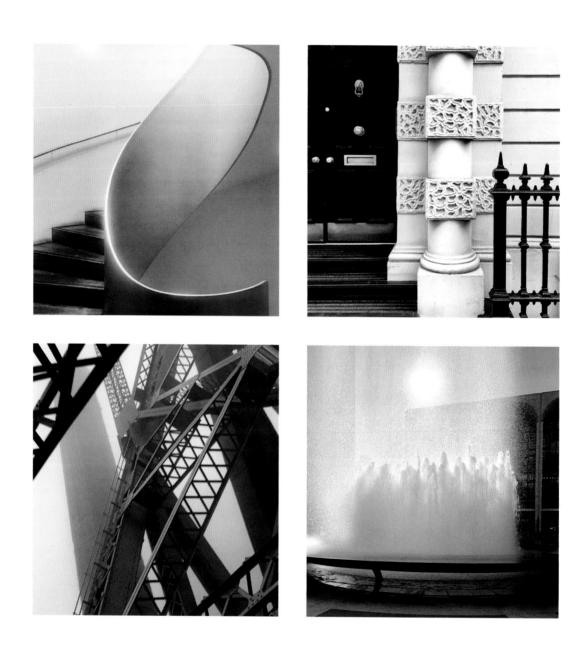

Paolo Buffa's teak, parchment, and brass mounted cabinet, c. 1940, sits beautifully under the stair in the entry. Hanging above it is a painting by Andisheh Avini, which mediates between the curve of the stair and the linearity of the cabinet.

went back to the same workroom, which meant all three pieces were made essentially by the same hand. To supplement this group, we found a fabulous 1950s-era chair and mixed it in with fauteuils they inherited. On the other side of the fireplace, we used his father's desk and desk chair to anchor another seating group. With an array of metals and a little Chinese table that came from her parents, the room represented a fresh, personal take on the generations.

We devised the dining room for both large occasions and more intimate, everyday use because the family eats together at the table every night. The paneled wall enhanced the room's functional aspects: the center doors concealed a bar; the side panels, glassware and dinnerware. The chandelier, by Jacques Jarrige, inserted a clear modern note into the traditional foundation. The mahogany and walnut Danish klismos chairs, c. 1850, were originally part of the royal inventory at Amalienborg Palace; because we needed a larger set, we had our cabinetmaker craft several others to match.

The L-shaped eat-in kitchen was designed for all-day use because we knew the children would hang out there with their friends or do homework. Including artwork such as the Le Corbusier lithographs over the kitchen table made this space both sophisticated and fun.

For the master bedroom, we created a haven washed in soft shades of blue. A subtle play of textures—linen, silk, velvet, and more—energized the quiet mood. Here, too, we incorporated family pieces, the bedside writing table among them.

With inherited pieces mixed in, this interior tells this family's story. The couple brought their families' past into their own present, combining them for the future. What could be more modern?

The living room sofa, which we recovered in velvet, belonged to her mother. We had chairs made by the same upholsterer to complete the seating group. Christopher Spitzmiller's table lamp is one of several metallic elements that add touches of gleam into this room. The drawing is by Jay Heikes.

Opposite: On the fireplace side of the living room, French styles overlap with a 1960s-era Charles Ramos–designed armchair, Maison Jansen coffee table, and Louis XVI-style fauteuils. Bernard Buffet's *Owl* hangs above the mantel. OVERLEAF, LEFT: The sunburst pattern of Alexandr Zhikulin's patinated-steel side table ties the room's elements together. OVERLEAF, RIGHT: With Charlotte Worthy, we streamlined the original mantel to bring it into proper scale for the room.

PRECEDING PAGES: These clients love to scout galleries, and they have a great eye. When they sent me photographs of the Jay Heikes drawing over the sofa and Matthias Bitzer's painting of a woman asking if they would work, I said, "Let's see." OPPOSITE: The inlaid rosewood cabinet is one of a pair designed by David Booth and Judith Ledeboer and made by Gordon Russell, Ltd. for the 1951 Festival of Britain. The drawing is by Diana Al-Hadid.

RIGHT AND OVERLEAF: We commissioned Keith Fritz to craft an extending dining table of French walnut with a sunburst top. The chairs around the table are a mix of Danish originals, c. 1850, from the royal inventory at the Amalienborg Palace and others made to match. By the windows are a pair from a second set, different in design but from the same period, purchased to add not only function but also visual interest. A brass chandelier by the hand of French artist Jacques Jarrige activates the space over the table, while a Helios lamp by Julien Barrault contributes another modern take on brass. The vintage Murano glass mirror dates to the 1940s.

Eero Saarinen's iconic pedastal table fits neatly into the kitchen dining nook, a magnet for the children and their friends to gather for fun, games, and homework. The subtle stripe of the settee fabric grounds the bursts of pattern and color in the lithographs by Le Corbusier that hang above. I love that these clients love art so much that they even include it in the kitchen.

In the master bedroom, we aimed to create a calm, restful atmosphere. A painting that she inherited from her father hangs above an antique writing table that was passed down from his grandmother. Everything else in the room is simple and understated in the viewing, but luxurious to the touch and rich in subtle complexities.

PERSONAL DETAILS

I love buying art for clients. But with clients like these who really enjoy the process of searching out artwork and artists, it is a treat for us to create rooms and backdrops, and then have these artistic elements show up as surprises. As we were working on this apartment, they would send me photos of paintings they had come across in galleries to get my opinion. My response was always, "Bring them home and see if you fall in love with them."

Bernard Buffet's *Owl* over the fireplace, though, was different because it was a favorite of hers from childhood. Her father, she explained, had purchased it on a trip to Paris in the late 1960s. When she asked if we could make it work, of course I was all for it. That it meant so much

to her made it extra special for me. And the fact that it was so unexpected made it the best kind of design challenge. But the canvas also struck a personal note for me. It reminded me of my mother, who believed that owls were signs of good fortune.

And so the painting became the inspiration for the entire scheme of the apartment. The most obvious riff on it was the decoration of the living room. Though I would never deliberately match a room's color palette to an artwork, I am sure the Buffet subconsciously affected my own decisions about color because I knew the painting would be a prominent part of the room. That said, there was also this wisdom of the owl: the client happened to love those hues, too.

HISTORY

It is impossible to appreciate something—anything—in detail unless we know how and why it came to be. Hence my fascination with history, and especially the history of design and the decorative arts. In interiors, as in life, looks enchant. But the backstory is what gives a piece of furniture or an object its deeper meaning. The idea that the things we make reflect the concerns and politics of the times in which we make them runs through our understanding of material culture. Knowing the conditions that led to the emergence of a particular form and type of object in a particular place at a particular time—and having a grasp on what else was coming to the fore elsewhere at the same time—helps us trace the evolution of civilization and culture.

From the dawn of time, we humans have been on the move. And because wherever we go, there we are, the things we make and bring with us have morphed not only over time, but also from shared influences. Just think about the development of American furniture. In our country's early years, furniture makers tended to copy what was being produced in England, France, or elsewhere. As they did, they put their own spin on things. This is not unlike what we do now. In this way, furniture is fashion.

Good design, though, has always been about function first. Chairs, tables, sideboards, desks, and so on all exist for a purpose, to address a need. Craftspeople have always appreciated what their pieces looked like and the work and expense that went into making them, as well as what they symbolized, and the ceremonies and rituals they served. In the history of furniture before the advent of mass production, very few pieces, however

My show house rooms often include furnishings and objects from my own collection. In this plaster copy of a life-size marble bust of Marquis de Lafayette by Jean-Antoine Houdon, Lafayette wears the medal of the Society of Cincinnati. The trim on the curtain panels, "Maria Tape," is named for the great Maria Callas; it is hand sewn with gemstones in India for F. Schumacher.

ornate, have been wasteful either in terms of materials or purpose.

I always try to trace the influences in any design I see, to peel back history in order to understand it. I want to figure out what led to what I am looking at and how it compares to similar types made in other places during the same period. This is one reason why I travel as much as I do. Another reason is that, for me, seeing with my own eyes, rather than through a screen or on a page, is believing. The word patina comes to mind. Patina, the palpable effect of time, is what separates the two viewing experiences. Both are valid, but it is impossible to truly get a feel for the quality of something—a city, an interior, a piece of furniture, a work of art—without experiencing it in person.

The pursuit of quality has always been part of human nature in one way or another. In terms of design and the decorative arts, quality is clearly the result of a thought process, not necessarily of expense or complexity. It can be expressed simply in the form of a silhouette, a shape, or a finish. But the ability to see it starts with exposure.

There is an interesting tension between timeliness and timelessness, between self-conscious decoration and enduring elegance. The great English country houses, for many of us, epitomize the latter. Their rooms are the result of accretion over time, education, and developed taste, with pieces from all periods of history and every place of origin. As generation after generation took the Grand Tour, they collected objects along the way and brought them home—a reflection of the learning process and the discernment that comes with it. We know when and how these rooms were created. We still want to savor the experience of being in them. They were, and are, about comfort, interest, and aesthetic appreciation.

Even today, it is travel and the building of experiences that bring furnishings and objects from different periods and styles harmoniously into a house. The mix is the central challenge for the designer. When we study and embrace the history of furniture, interiors, and the decorative arts in general, everything falls into line. The best interiors are those with meaning, whether the meaning lies in the choice and arrangement of objects, the quality of the space, or the character and details of the lifestyle.

Every person has a different history, and a specific set of wants and needs. The first house I did on my own as a designer was a place in the Hamptons for a British client. She appreciated antiques, so we searched high and low for pieces from all different areas and time periods, everything from Anglo-Indian to Egyptian. When I visit the house with her now, we talk about each item. We recall what we were doing the day we found it, and where we had lunch, who was with us, what the weather was like. We can remember who the dealer was and the knowledge that the dealer shared: that the artisan who made the piece had to find just the right piece of timber, for example, and match the grain on two sides. With every piece we purchased, we learned to look deeper and appreciate more. The house was empty when we began. Now it is full of meaning—and pieces her grandchildren will treasure.

There is also much to be said about a crisp new interior. Antiques call for a level of commitment to the future. They have survived for centuries and brought joy to those who care, so their current owners have a responsibility to keep them safe and sound for the next. But sometimes people want to simplify their lives, to live with pieces they do not have to worry about, to experience their rooms afresh, to cleanse their palates. That urge has nothing to do with the objects per se. It can be about the desire to live in an open space. Or it can be about the wish to start the next chapter, to build a different history. Every antique was new once. Every new piece will be old one day if it is of quality.

The now does not come out of a bubble. Appreciating the old leads us to the modern. One does not exist without the other. I love that we can play detective with every little piece, that we can know why and how the path has led us here. True invention is very rare.

OVERLEAF: For this room in Holiday House, a show house benefiting breast cancer research, we emphasized layers of history with designs from different periods and countries. The console and side chairs are English Regency, contrasting with the contemporary French bronze globe chandelier. Contemporary artwork includes Curtis Jeré's sculpture on the coffee table, an Emilia Dubicki painting above the sofa, and a painting by Victor-Raul Garcia over the fireplace.

PRECEDING PAGES: A Regency mahogany table from the 1820s (left) supports all sorts of objects. Atop one of the consoles is a Charles X clock from 1825 (right).
OPPOSITE: Masatoyo Kishi's gestural stone bird suggests the element of flight in the window.

This room is also an ode to two other historic moments: the 125th anniversary of F. Schumacher & Co. and the 25th anniversary of *Traditional Home* magazine, one of the Holiday House sponsors. Elements from all my favorite eras represent the evolution of design from Regency to today. The contingent from the Regency, always one of my top five, includes this voluptuous-yet-disciplined mahogany sofa. Adding a moment of whimsy to the mix is a pair of sheep, from the 1970s, in the manner of Lalanne.

Always, the threads of history spool in interesting directions. This armchair, by Edward Wormley for Dunbar, dates to the 1950s. It is a reference to David Easton, who worked in Wormley's office before launching his own firm. The standing lamp by Clodagh, the Irish-born designer, nods to my own Irish heritage. The hurricane candle light is by Anasthasia Millot.

FAMILY HISTORY

Some houses just feel meant to be. Others, especially when newly built, need love and attention to make them that way. This house is the second kind. When these longtime clients purchased it, it had good bones but lacked any sense of architectural style or focus. To fill it with the welcoming living spaces they envisioned, they knew they needed the backgrounds that only good architecture provides. Before we started to build up the decoration, we worked to correct what existed not just by adding ceiling beams, wall panel details, moldings, and mantels, but also by fine-tuning each element to get its scale, profile, and silhouettes right.

The original two-story entry was vast. Central to the life of the house, it acted as the mediator between the interior's public areas—darker, richer, and antique filled, without going too formal—and its private spaces—lighter, with more modern choices. Arches, overhangs, moldings, and baseboards transformed the character of the entry. Covering the walls in an Anglo-Indian—inspired damask wallpaper—traditional, but not fussy, a little stylized, but not self-conscious—introduced the necessary warmth and a more intimate scale. Red felt like the perfect color to walk into, and this particular shade was just the right hue to pull together the interior's different sections.

One of design's most wonderful paradoxes is how the new can imbue a space with history. In this entry hall, carefully considered wood detailing, an Anglo-Indian Victorian-style paper from Carleton V, a custom corner chair created on instinct, and an Irish landscape, c. 1860, establish a sense of timeliness and timelessness.

In the living room, a medium-dark palette felt appropriate, mainly because they use this room at night. Balanced by luminous velvets, touches of understated pattern, and the gleam of gilded and polished finishes, the duskier tones made for glamorous surroundings enhanced by the antiques and artwork they love.

The original library was a dim, paneled cave of a space. Instead of replacing the existing wood, which was not particularly beautiful, we decided to paint it. The saturated hue we chose, though still deep and rich, gave the room a younger, fresher feel.

The family kitchen, which includes family dining and sitting areas, defined the other end of the spectrum. These rooms opened onto outdoor terraces, the backyard, and the pool. Soft, pale palettes and more contemporary furnishings made them feel airy, relaxed, and organically connected to the exterior.

The pantry and its adjacent areas are heavily trafficked, so they needed to blend in organically with the rest of the decor. Because the family entertains friends often and hosts all the family functions—their children also love to come home on weekends—we designed unique storage and outfitted antiques to house their expansive collections.

These clients have always embraced the idea of pretty, especially in the bedrooms, whether the master suite or the guest rooms. Wrapped in floral wallpaper and dressed in lovely fabrics, each became its own secret garden.

When a house has been well loved and well used, whether old or new, it reveals its unique history. Nothing in this one looks crisp and brand new, even though, technically, everything is. The velvet on the chairs is worn because people have sat in the chairs, used them during pizza parties and for watching hockey games. For this family, a home is meant to enhance the pleasure of the family life it houses. And nothing is off limits.

OPPOSITE: On the entry hall's other side, a c. 1870 case clock made in Thurso, Scotland, and English Regency chairs, c. 1820, round out the British invasion. OVERLEAF: New soffits organize this long living room into three sections. Sisal flooring balances pieces from many periods, including painted Continental side chairs, c. 1880.

JESSICA and LORENZO.

ROSILAND, CELIA & ORLANDO.

PRECEDING PAGES: In the gallery leading to the husband's office/library/TV room and the living room, a nineteenth-century wing chair sits neatly in one corner. Above is a pair of late eighteenth-century English reverse paintings on glass that depict Shakespearean characters. OPPOSITE: To introduce symmetry and glamour in the living room, we flanked the entry with mirror-image L-shaped banquettes in velvet and midcentury brass tables, c. 1950. OVERLEAF, LEFT: An antique Italian gilt bullseye mirror, c. 1910, brings focus to a wall between French doors. OVERLEAF, RIGHT: French art deco sconces with verdigris-finished frames and gilt Egyptian-influenced details and Louis XVI-style photophores on the mantel add to the layering of history in the room.

I love chairs for so many reasons. From a designer's perspective, of course, they are functional, practical, and necessary for comfort. But they are also such intriguing sculptural forms.

RIGHT: At the far end of the living room, French doors offer views and easy access into the landscape. OVERLEAF: A deep English armchair offers an invitation to lounge. Behind is a brass etagère with black opaline shelves that show off a collection of white earthenware and blanc de chine pieces. Antique books are lovely for literary reasons. They are also beautiful objects that lend a great deal of visual texture.

OPPOSITE: Bronze curtain poles run through the entire house. In the breakfast room, contemporary chairs mix with a late Regency cane design, c. 1820, around a nineteenth-century table. We found the vintage lantern in Dublin. OVERLEAF: In the kitchen sitting room, a tall vase by Frances Palmer, the Connecticut-based potter and a longtime family friend, completes the grouping of meaningful pieces on the mantel. An English Regency mirror introduces a note of elegant whimsy. An extra-wide chair is a comfortable place to lounge and chat while meals are being prepared.

OPPOSITE: In keeping with the overall style of these interiors, a custom cupboard for the collection of platters by Frances Palmer commands a wall in an area adjacent to the pantry. OVERLEAF: George Smith's Edwardian chairs suit the spirit of the husband's office/library/TV room. Pierre Vandel's coffee table, c. 1970, is a light touch among more solid elements. Shawn Snow's landscape hangs between windows.

Lighting is always important to the surroundings. Here, we made sure to have indirect lamp lighting below eye level both for reading and to set a quiet, intimate mood. Granite-topped side tables by Jonathan Burden provide great perches for books and interesting objects.

The couple entertains frequently, so we placed a bar off the gallery between the living room and the husband's office/library/TV room. In this part of the house, the style veers into a more modern mode and the colors grow more saturated. A Macassar ebony bar credenza by Maurice Rinck, c. 1940, does double duty for storage and display below a painting by Emilia Dubicki.

RIGHT AND OVERLEAF: The wife is not afraid of pretty. Nor am I. And she has always had a special fondness for beautiful floral wallpaper, which gives me such pleasure. Strange as it may seem, it is difficult these days to find them. This one is English. The bedside lamps complement the soft palette and floral motifs of the wallpaper.

THREADS OF TIME

When we choose the soft and hard components of decoration, we use the same senses and critical faculties. But the priorities differ. With furniture, the eye is the first responder, assessing form, line, and silhouette, and whether the piece fits the function. With textiles, touch takes precedence. We react viscerally to how the different fibers and textures feel against our skin.

Creating a room that feels lived in calls for more than just new elements, no matter how beautiful. One piece of antique furniture can add so much personality. Vintage and antique fabrics weave in texture and style, and the depth that history brings.

These clients love fine old things. We all fell in love with this antique pillow, from designer Rebecca Vizard, as much for the story behind it as its look and feel. The embroidery's open pattern contrasted well with the aged thread's texture and character; the scale and detail of the design balanced well with the room's other elements.

Rebecca told us she salvaged the gold work from a very distressed nineteenth-century Ottoman Empire *bohça* she found in Turkey. We learned that a *bohça*—the word means "to wrap" or "wrapper"—is a square of fabric, usually velvet or silk, about the size of a bridge table cover, with embroidery in the center and on all four corners. People used these special cloths to protect their valuables in transport, putting cherished items in the center of the textile, then folding each corner over to wrap them up in a tidy package.

Here, on a new velvet ground, in a different role and environment, this handiwork of history endures and continues to enhance the lives it touches.

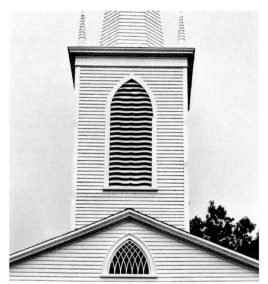

SURROUNDINGS

It seems so simple to say that design and decoration should reflect location. Yet there is so much more to the nature of a place than coordinates on a map. Obviously, geography matters. But perhaps more important are the quality of the light, the degree of seasonal change, the character of the surroundings, whether urban or mountain, suburban or seaside. Every aspect of the world beyond our walls and windows can and should affect our choices within them—everything from architecture to materials, fabrics, and finishes to color palettes and types and styles of furnishings. What looks good and right in Paris or London does not necessarily have the same power of persuasion in Manhattan, Palm Beach, or San Francisco. The differences can be subtle. But they are real. And as with everything in life, they change over time.

I love the fantasies that interior design can evoke. Yet the concept of "Versailles in the Sky"—a Louis XVI–style gilded lily of a living space hovering atop a glass tower—feels dissonant, a home out of balance with its surroundings. This is why appropriateness drives so much of my decision-making process. I can still remember the old days of windows overlooking the ocean festooned with swags and jabots. Of beachside houses with suits of armor poised like greeters in the entry hall. Of society column pictures of fur-coated ladies bedazzled with tiaras under palm trees. Today, fortunately, these are exceptions.

Warmer and colder climates call for different sensibilities in terms of the elements of decor. In regions where sunshine and high temperatures tend to be constant, paler colors and weightless linens can make an

The light reflecting off the Gulf of Mexico factored into all the choices for the interiors of this house in Naples, Florida. Patterns and colors for the most part are very subtle. But the more the eye focuses, the more the different textures come to the fore. The hall painting is by John Schuyler. The photograph is one of mine.

interior feel ethereal, easy, and breezy, whereas just contemplating a woolen or thick woven fabric can make one break a sweat. In areas where temperatures and weather swing substantially from one season to the next, there is a different mentality. And a different look. With fabrics, in particular, it is necessary to walk that fine line between what works both when the trees are in full bloom and when they are bare or snow-covered. And all the variations in between.

Light brings so much life to a room throughout the day, and throughout the year. It also varies in color, clarity, and intensity from place to place—city to city, region to region, country to country. I first noticed this years ago when I was working on a residence in San Francisco with a glorious view of the Bay. This client happened to have a very fine collection of Old Master paintings. The combination of these two givens pointed me in a certain direction for textures, materials, and color palettes. When I began the project, I thought I had put together such fabulous schemes. When I took the samples out to the site to be sure, I realized I had to rethink all my decisions because the quality of the light in the Bay Area was so different from that in Manhattan.

Where we are in the arc of our lives also has a profound impact on what we feel is appropriate for our domestic landscapes. When one of my clients, a longtime antiques dealer based in New England, migrated south to Naples, Florida, she brought her American antiques with her. When she saw that her bright, airy Florida surroundings did not lend themselves to rooms full of dark wood pieces, even though they had great personal and historical significance, she decided to hold onto just a few very favorite pieces and her paintings. Everything else we selected for her home was crisp, light, and contemporary.

People tend to use their vacation homes differently from their primary residences. A ski house presents one set of conditions for design and decoration; a beach house, another. How the homeowners entertain factors into the choices. Do they fill the house with friends every weekend or keep their gatherings more intimate and family-centric? All of which is to say that my principles of design do not change, but my sense of what will suit in terms of decor varies with the locale and the purpose of the house.

I am always looking at houses. I imagine myself living in different homes, locations, and environments around the world. On my phone, I keep weather updates for so many cities. Dublin is a constant, and it is always fifty-six degrees and raining. I keep an eye on Cork, too. But the Dingle Peninsula is the place that really calls to me. In my mind's eye, as in fact I know from experience, the environment is rugged. The fog, the mist, the cold, the damp—all make certain demands of the kind of rooms I picture myself happily inhabiting there. Sunshine, even though there must be plenty, is not part of the equation when I think about my house in Ireland that I do not have. I love the idea of one large room centered on a great, roaring fireplace. This place would not be terribly high style, just comfortable and relaxed. The walls would be soft in color because who does not want to come into warmth and light when the outside is so often moody and stormy? The furniture would be made for nesting, the kind to sink into for long stays because the weather ensures a lot of time spent indoors. There would be lots of books and well-placed reading lamps. And not one single piece to worry about when I leave and shut the door behind me.

Architecture always matters. It creates its own environment. If a house is appropriate for what it is, if it has sufficient character and respect for its location, it can feel just right for today—neither old, nor new, though it may be newly built. The way the architect sites the house, lays out the living spaces, and orients the rooms sets the stage for all the decorative decisions that follow. Certain places, certain structures, call for interiors of a certain style. The inside need not match the outside precisely. Far from it. But the interior should connect as much to its surroundings as it does to those who live within it, and at least nod to its location.

OPPOSITE: Interior columns define both space and function in the more open areas of this house. A linen-wrapped table centers the living room. A nineteenth-century Thai lamp and a ceramic bowl by Bob Pesce balance the straight lines with curves. OVERLEAF: This couple fell in love with a series of photographs on my Instagram page that captured favorite places in their travels. In the den, a basketweave shell pattern on the coffee table adds another layer of understated pattern, as well as a bit of sheen for contrast. The painting is by Karen Minges.

OPPOSITE The design of these indoor/outdoor pieces from Janus et Cie walk a fine line between traditional and contemporary. I think they fit anywhere and will never look dated. OVERLEAF: This sitting room between the kitchen and dining room is a wonderful spot for family and friends to relax while talking to whoever's cooking. Retracting glass doors open up to the dining patio. The painting over the sofa is by Holly Addi.

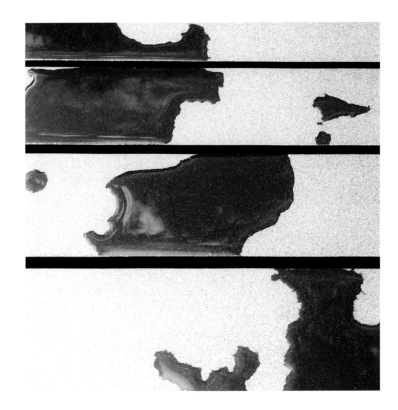

PRECEDING PAGES: To my eye, line and form combine to create overall visual harmony. OPPOSITE: In a coincidence that makes me smile, my photograph of my backyard table mirrors the painting by John Schuyler over the sofa in the office. An ebony coffee table by Walker Zabriskie reflects traditional Asian design.

For consistency, we decided to use the coffee table version of the Janus et Cie dining table design to anchor the lounge on the terrace. Basketweave furniture picks up on the elements of rattan in other areas of the house. The fabrics are indoor/outdoor blends for ease and comfort.

SENSE OF PLACE

Sometimes it is impossible to renovate a great, quirky old house to work for today's lifestyle, no matter how much everyone loves it. That was the story here. Fortunately, it ends happily in a new house designed by architect Peter Pennoyer. The replacement resonates with the feeling and generous spirit of the original, a rambling early twentieth-century shingle-style cottage on the water, even as it translates and updates the original's eccentricities and key features, including a fantastic columned porch. It also incorporates some architectural elements and details salvaged from the teardown, which makes such a difference. Now usable all year round, the place works perfectly. All the spaces are much more open to a landscape, by designer Edwina von Gal, that looks as if it has always been there, and to the spectacular ocean views. The rooms function beautifully and flow together seamlessly. The kitchen, once an afterthought, is just right for this young family and their visiting family and friends.

This couple loves interesting, unique things, so we put together a mix of elements and furnishings as eclectic as their tastes. They treasure the pieces they brought back from Asia, where they lived for five years. They travel often, and they have a special fondness for France. They care for the summer-house classics, such as the wicker furniture, left behind by the house's previous owner, that we spruced up and reused. They have an eye for pattern, which travels, subtly, throughout the house, ensuring the rooms look warm and inviting even when there is snow on the ground, the branches are bare, and the winter sky is heavy and gray.

In the living room, the textures and materials span a wide spectrum. Light filters through woven window shades. Blown-glass table lamps insert notes of shine and reflection. A seating group centers on a cocktail table made from two benches topped by tufted cushions set in resin.

The bookcase-lined dining room is at the heart of the house. The children like to do their homework at the table, so it is often covered with books and laptops. She made the wonderful suggestion of using a bold pattern on the chair backs. This key feature of the room brings the environment to life for those entering or looking through in passing.

OPPOSITE: The husband's office is just off the master bedroom on the second floor; the Dutch door, true to the original architecture, leads to a terrace overlooking the water. A Bruno Romeda stool offers a handy surface next to the desk. OVERLEAF: The window fabric inspired the living room, which harmonizes many textures and periods. The nineteenth-century Chinese cabinet, one of the first pieces we found, brings to mind their time in Asia.

OPPOSITE: Woven shades give the living room a casual feel and blend naturally with the Asian elements; they also filter the light beautifully. Inspired by the form of the classic fauteuil, these chairs from Lucca Antiques in Los Angeles are a modern take on tradition. OVERLEAF: At the core of the house, the dining room opens to many rooms. Chair backs upholstered with a bold pattern create captivating views for those looking into the space from all angles. An antique Agra carpet continues the pattern and color story underfoot. We had the table handmade to fit the room's look and dimensions.

The textures and colors in the master suite draw inspiration from the surroundings, with suggestions of soft sand and hues that pull from the sea and sky. Her desk, a curved Jansen piece from the 1940s, occupies the bay opposite the bed to take advantage of the view. His office nests in an adjacent alcove.

This couple are avid readers, and their passion for the printed word makes the guest bedroom a special place, with bookcases that hold a complete series of Penguin Classics. The fabrics and wallcoverings also have personal meaning, as we custom colored some and worked closely with the designers of others.

Year after year, these rooms evolve. The dining room bookcases reflect how life proceeds. Children's board and picture books have slowly given way to chapter books and young adult fiction. Mementos from recent family trips mix in with the older treasures. Summer trophies from the beach and rainy-day art projects chart the seasons—the kind of changes that every family, and every house, welcomes.

PRECEDING PAGES: The kitchen is architect Peter Pennoyer's design; it relates to the original but is all about today. We salvaged this sink from the original house. The objects above tell the same period story, with a drawing by Bill Goldsmith, an eighteenth-century ship diorama, and eighteenth- and nineteenth-century American pottery. OPPOSITE: The back stair connects to the kitchen. Portholes in the stairwell bring light from the skylight into the children's rooms.

PRECEDING PAGES: The master suite swims with light and takes ultimate advantage of the views. Anthony Lawrence-Belfair, responsible for upholstery and curtains throughout, fabricated the bed hangings from my Beatrice Bouquet design for Schumacher. A pair of Swedish bed tables, c. 1820, adds another layer of texture and age. The clients purchased the fourteenth-century Laotian drum in Asia. Her lacquered desk, a curved Jansen design, fits perfectly into the bay. The painting is by Victor-Raul Garcia.

RIGHT: These clients relate to patterns and fabrics, a joy for me. Dennis Lee of Tyler Hall designed the custom-colored pattern called Bloomsbury that covers the guest bedroom's walls. The wicker sofa, original to the house, by chance fit perfectly in the window niche. The window fabric is one of Katie Leede's.

PRECEDING PAGES: With its painted floor and ceiling, black wicker furniture, and vintage bench, the porch captures the spirit of the old house. The onion fixtures overhead resemble ship lights. OPPOSITE: Edwina von Gal's landscaping is simple, and perfect. She conceived the minimalist pool and its position on axis with the view. As the plantings have grown in, they feel as if they have been here forever. Classic Adirondack chairs mixed with more contemporary pieces reinforce the idea of design as a continuum in time.

THE FRENCH CONNECTION

So much of design is finding the delicate balance among all the various parts of a vignette, a corner, a room, or a home. The calculus of what stands out, what remains quiet, and what harmonizes in ways that draw and please the eye without overwhelming it is different for every person, occasion, space, and function. This couple has a very eclectic point of view. They travel widely. But they also have certain favorite destinations, like France, as the pieces we put together in their breakfast area make clear.

When I am in Paris, I make it a habit on Saturdays to go to the Marché aux Puces de Clignancourt, where I enjoy running into fellow designers and comparing notes. But the best part, always, is the hunt. This pair of vintage bistro tables, which date to about 1935 and come from a café in Marseilles, was one of our lucky finds, in part because of their unexpectedly good proportions, deep enough and wide enough to be comfortable instead of cramped. While the oak tops and chrome details needed freshening up, we made sure not to over-restore them because we wanted to respect their history. The café tables also relate particularly well to the late nineteenth-century French frame above the banquette. The tiles tell the story of this piece, which was made for a fish market in Paris and originally had a blackboard to note the daily catch in its central section. I usually prefer not to be so obvious in what we select to pair, but I just could not resist the charm created when these elements came together, or how they seemed so right for this particular corner of this house by the sea.

DRAMA

I love the theater. While I do not believe that all the world's a stage and we are all merely players, I find the complex relationship between what we imagine for the stage, and what we experience off it to be endlessly fascinating. Whether intimate or operatic, a one-person show or a DeMille-sized cast of thousands, drama and comedy have an unparalleled power to tell stories and reveal human truths. From a design perspective, everything on the stage has a purpose. Sets and costumes, lighting and choreography—all have to work to help propel the narrative. That is why it is rare to see a stage dressed in some weird fantasy that has nothing to do with the world it is meant to frame. At best, the backgrounds illuminate and reflect the personalities of those "people" who live in that space, at that time. This need for purposeful expression plays into everything that interior designers do. I always try to figure out how my clients would like to live: to understand how they see themselves, how they want to see themselves, how they want other people to see them, and what kinds of spaces would give them pleasure and make them feel comfortable and at home.

The first play I ever saw on Broadway was *Much Ado About Nothing* starring Sam Waterston and Kathleen Widdoes. A. J. Antoon, the director, had set the action in pre–World War I Middle America. The show had ragtime music. And Keystone Kops. And a merry-go-round. I can still conjure up individual scenes in my mind's eye. That night in the theater is when I first became aware of lighting and the tricks it can create. I remember having a flash of insight about how everything on a stage can come together to project a singular, specific world.

In this corner of the main living/dining space in this Tribeca loft, patterns, textures, and influences from around the world convene. A tribal antelope mask found in London surveys a stylized animal print on a neoclassical klismos chair from atop a painted, 1930s-era French gueridon table.

When I was studying at FIT and living at the YMCA on 63rd Street, I was lucky to become friends with some young people from London, one of whom was the assistant to John Dexter. At the time, Mr. Dexter was the director of production for the Metropolitan Opera. While he was in London on a visit, he let us hang out at his apartment, which was full of maquettes of his sets for Dialogues des Carmélites, the Poulenc opera. His vision was so spare. So beautiful. So effective—essentially a cruciform platform spanning a raked stage. Its opening and closing images—of nuns lying prostrate on that cross, and of walking single file to their death by guillotine—haunt everyone I know who has seen it.

It amazes me how creative set designers can be, and sometimes with so little. This is a lesson well learned about the potential of even the smallest gesture. At the Kips Bay Decorator Show House years ago, I had the dining room, always one of my favorite spaces to design. This one, though, was entirely paneled in a Chinese scenic wallcovering that had seen better days. It presented a formidable challenge because we were not allowed to remove it. Even more difficult than that, we were not even permitted to touch its surface. At first, I was stuck. Then I thought, "You were a theater major once. You have seen enough theater that you can figure out what to do." First, I decided the ideal solution would be to frame out the wallpaper panels. Fortunately, the room had prominent crown moldings and baseboards. I built inverted, L-shaped wood braces that we mounted serially around the room, Velcroing them top and bottom to the flat area of the crown molding and the body of the baseboard. (The braces never touched the wall or the paper.) Then we tacked an inexpensive fabric, about eight dollars per yard, to each of the braces, creating an entirely new paneled background. That is theater, in its way. But more importantly it, it is the result of reacting to a space and thinking, "What else can I do?" Everything we see and experience—all of our inspiration— adds up to the way we approach individual solutions.

In a house, design and decoration can take infinite different directions. Yet individual rooms have their own underlying character and purpose. Dining rooms and powder rooms should be dramatic and glamorous. There are so many great elements for creating a wonderfully rich and evocative environment: the dining table and the chairs, the chandelier, sconces, sideboards, artwork, window treatments. Because each chair at the table faces a slightly different view, I am conscious of what the room looks like from every angle, from every side, and from every seat. Lighting is key, and I always try to make sure that no light spills in from any adjacent rooms to ruin the mood.

Every room in the house is its own little theater-in-the-round. But dining rooms for me are more so, and thus they are the perfect place for a bold color statement. Even when the preference is for light neutrals or all white, I will make sure that I have created moments to draw and delight the eye, moments that make the room memorable. I might add a graphic pattern in a high-contrast color to the chair backs and select the rug carefully to create a visual punch on entry. And because people today tend to stay at the table and talk when dinner is done, the dining chairs have to be very comfortable.

The tabletop is a stage in miniature, and so much fun to set. Tableware, glassware, flatware, linens, flowers, candlesticks, and other ornaments offer endless opportunities for creating character and a sense of occasion. Elaborate china, silver, and glassware tell one story. Pared-down pieces tell another. One beautifully ornamented object on a plain tablecloth becomes more special by contrast. Or vice versa.

How can any designer not love theater? Yes, it exists on a different scale than those we work in every day. But it teaches when and how to turn the visual volume up and down depending on the scenario. Theater stretches the mind. It makes us think, and think outside the box. It makes us appreciate other designers. Most of all, it reminds us of the power of the imagination and the role design and decoration have in making the pieces we live with and the rooms we live in more interesting, surprising, comfortable, and individual.

The freestanding furnishings in this room hug the walls, rather like a ship. This is not my usual approach to furniture planning, but it makes sense here because this space in a former factory is quite narrow. The carved paws on the overscaled Belgian ottoman pick up on the animal motif. Peter Margonelli photographed a bride through the shop window of a photo studio in Mumbai; blowing up the image and subdividing it into sections creates a dramatic focal point.

The painting by Edgar Buonagurio comments on the mysterious mottling of Peter Margonelli's photograph. The willow wood cabinet, c. 1900, was carved with tribal patterns in Shing Jiang province, the gateway to the original Marco Polo trail. With numerous rooms and pieces from many different periods and places, Benjamin Moore's "Notre Dame" establishes a visual throughline.

In shades of pale neutrals, the Schumacher ikat on
both seating groups quietly stands out against the dark
walls and reinforces the exoticism that ties together
the mix of elements. The ottoman's oversized paws
remind me of Anglo-Indian detailing on favorite
pieces seen over the years. Over the sofa is an intricate,
French-Indonesian pierced mirror that pulls the
curves and angles of the ikat pattern up onto the wall.
Spots of red draw the eye around the room.

OPPOSITE: The wall pattern in the dining room pieces together elements of four different Schumacher wallpapers. The vibe of a plaster mirror and Arbus-style dining chairs from the 1940s work with an Anglo-Indian column, c. 1860, one of a pair that stand like exclamation points in the corners of the room. OVERLEAF: In his office, a painting by Beatrice Caracciolo brings in a touch of modern to the shelf display. His desk features a top by Alpha Workshops resting on a zinc drum cut in half and formed into an S-curve. A leaf-covered wallpaper from Hermès brings in a 1940s sensibility.

PRECEDING PAGES: Having looked at this nineteenth-century door frame in a Connecticut shop for years and imagined all different ways to use it, this bedroom was the perfect fit. A 1920s view of Venice floats atop a gray mirror inserted in the door frame. OPPOSITE: A 1981 photograph by Gerald Incandela of Rodin's bust of Balzac adds another visual dimension to the classical elements of the room. OVERLEAF: Julian Schnabel's wall-sized painting makes a statement with a George III armchair in gaufrage velvet.

OPPOSITE AND OVERLEAF: There is something about strong, saturated colors, and contrast that reads particularly well through the lens, especially in images of the landscape. This realization has influenced my design choices over time, both consciously and unconsciously. This Park Avenue library reflects some of that evolution. Removing the old, heavy paneling, adding moldings and a stepped ceiling with the help of architect Charlotte Worthy, and finishing the walls in a deep, light-reflective blue were instrumental in refreshing the space. Between the windows is a work in mixed media on paper by Richard Diebenkorn.

Lamps by Jacques Jarrige and sconces by Jules Leleu infuse the library with French accents. The Chinese low table is made of jumu wood and dates to about 1910. With its pronounced geometric pattern, the carpet lays an orderly foundation. Above the sofa hangs a painting by Oscar Murillo.

The clients inherited the early eighteenth-century Queen Anne bureau bookcase from the wife's grandmother, who had a distinguished collection of English furniture. A Japanese lacquer trunk introduces a contained burst of a more intricate pattern at a contrasting scale.

NEW BEGINNINGS

Every design project is a test of skill and imagination. But some projects challenge a designer to think beyond the norm in really interesting ways. This house on Long Island Sound is one of them. It is not a summer house. And it is not a winter house. In other words, the rooms needed to be warm, welcoming, and intimate for all four seasons. And because the house is surrounded by water and very exposed to the elements, we had to take all practical matters, such as protecting the furniture from harsh daylight and salt air, into account from the beginning.

This couple, newly married, started building the home and its interiors from scratch. Happily, they were both good decision makers who agreed on what they liked. They appreciated the comfort of well-made upholstery. They loved beautiful fabrics. Best of all from my point of view, they did not want to live in a house without antiques. As we shopped, they responded to clean-lined, classic pieces with a stylized Regency look. They also had an eye for antique Oriental carpets, which we used in the entry hall and the dining room. These older rugs helped balance out the contemporary handmade carpets we used elsewhere, adding a layer of depth and history.

OPPOSITE: The close-patterned Karabagh carpet, c. 1885, lays a foundation of age in the entry hall of this newly built house in Greenwich. A Russian tilt-top table, c. 1780-1800, enhances the feeling of history. The contemporary bench introduces a luxurious combination of bronze, brass, and leather. OVERLEAF: In a square room, using as many different curves as possible helps to soften the edges. The Piermont armchairs and sofas from Jonas Upholstery have such appealing silhouettes, and their forms relate to all the other pieces. It is also very unusual to find sofas of this size with wood trim. Resting on the mantel are drawings by Toko Shinoda.

A 1940s ebonized demi-lune console is in keeping not only with the other
neoclassical pieces, but also with its more contemporary components.
The Chinese red porcelain vase from Henan Province, c. 1930, is timeless.

A bronze-and-glass coffee table anchors the living room's primary seating area; these materials help draw and move the light through the space. Many of the fabrics here also have a slight reflective sheen. The water-colored palette takes its inspiration from the views.

The dining room had some of the best views in the house, with magnificent sunsets year round, but especially in the summer. Because the room was vast, dark walls made it feel more intimate. Pale fabrics and artwork balanced the deep tones, ensuring the room also looked great during the daytime. For seating, we searched out the most comfortable upholstered chairs we could find because the couple knew their guests preferred to sit at the table as long as possible rather than returning to the living room after the meal.

Shades of off-white, soft grays, and some brown thread their way through the interior. In the living room, sofas upholstered in a deep sable-colored velvet anchored the seating area; luxurious, soft, and texturally interesting, the fabric does wonderful things with light. To keep the room from feeling too staid, we also added touches of red, my go-to color for sparking interest and moving the eye around the room. Because it turns out that red leather is the first thing to fade, we made little slipcovers for the stools. Unless the couple expects guests, these protective covers stay on during the day.

This couple travels frequently. Wherever they find themselves, they enjoy going to galleries and searching out mementos of their trips. And they always return with a picture, a painting, a drawing. There is a wonderful Christian Bérard over the mantel that they found on a recent trip to Paris. On their next trip there, I made sure they visited La Méditerranée, a treasure of a restaurant with murals painted by Bérard— another place where life meets art, and another layer of memories to bring home.

The Louis XVI-style painted bench fits beautifully in the window, a perfect spot to daydream or to contemplate the moods of the light and sea as they change hour by hour through the seasons.

The New English Garden

Outstanding American Gardens

This couple has an eye for antiques with beautiful lines, including this mahogany center table made in Philadelphia, c. 1820. Antique Chinese vases on the tabletop bring the colors of the water inside. The leather-upholstered stools are by Jacques Adnet, c. 1940.

PRECEDING PAGES: In the dining room, the silvered arms of the Ruhlmann-style chandelier complement the different tones of silver in the room, including the silver-papered ceiling. A nineteenth-century English mantel in white stone boldly frames the fireplace. A watercolor by Christian Bérard commands attention on the mantel. A pair of banquettes flank the fireplace; above each hangs a painting by Caio Fonseca. OPPOSITE: The gilded nineteenth-century mirror that anchors one wall of the dining room was chosen because its reeded detailing relates so well to the panels of the console below it.

SIGHT LINES

In my view, just about every interior can benefit from some "brown furniture." When we order everything new from showrooms, the rooms that result can be very beautiful. But they are also predictable. We know ahead of time what they will look like when they are finished. Antiques and vintage pieces add the element of surprise, as well as depth, history, and personality. And so much of antiquing is luck, a matter of being in the right place at the right time—and of what is in the market—which is what makes the hunt so much fun.

This dining room wall was visible from the front door, a focal point that called for something special to anchor the view from the entry. I envisioned a piece—a console or a cabinet, nothing too jazzy or flashy—that could stand on its own in terms of visual heft and also work with the room's proportions and the decoration we had planned.

On one of my usual scouting trips through the antiques galleries, I had seen a late Regency mahogany console. Ever since that first sighting, I had kept my eye on it. Regency furniture was my first love, and the reason all those years ago that I had wanted to work for David Easton, who shared a fondness for the style. This console exemplifies the period. Based on designs by the English cabinetmaker George Smith, it dates to circa 1825.

When the clients and I first looked at it together, they responded with an immediate yes. I was thrilled for them—and so glad the piece had found its next home.

ATMOSPHERE

Think of walking into a Gothic cathedral or the Oculus, Santiago Calatrava's white whale of a transportation hub in Lower Manhattan, or, at a more human scale, a house. What do such different spaces share? A distinctive quality of light. A unique form and particular volume. Wondrous architecture. The thrill of decoration. Spaces can inspire awe. They can give you goose bumps. They can comfort. They can instill a sense of home. Whatever the feelings they engender, the cause is always atmosphere—or, if you prefer, mood or ambience. Atmosphere is the word so many of us use to describe the indescribable: that elusive quality we experience within a specific space, at a specific time, in a specific place.

I was very influenced by old Hollywood movies growing up. For me, the images on the screen, more often than not in black and white, were always about light. There were the shadows cast by shutters, ominous or peaceful or energizing. There were the lace patterns from the curtains silhouetted on the walls, cloying or joyful or elegant. No matter what, it was clear in these old films that what defined home were those shafts of light coming through the windows.

Movies are one thing; living spaces, another. The mood of the living space, unlike those of the movies, does not need to be full of import in order to be glamorous. Rooms can be simple in spirit. Or not. And they can change. But ambience created by design and decoration is intrinsic to what makes every room unique, and the moments within it memorable. The reasons behind the choices matter. And they are why we focus on atmosphere. When everything within the room calls out for attention,

Design can echo time and taste in interesting, sometimes magical ways. An eighteenth-century Italian mirror over the mantel shows its age with such grace, adding an air of mystery through its mottled silver-gilt frame. Around the table is a set of Louis XVI-style armchairs by Jansen that come from an apartment decorated by Henri Samuel.

nerves tend to jangle. For some, the experience is very moving. For me, there can be too much "wow."

As a designer, I find that what stands out in every room are the quiet moments, the understated but beautiful elements that also function beautifully, in part by allowing other pieces to shine. The coffee table may be a Parsons table or a modest Chinese table, but its presence is enhanced when it serves as a showplace for the interesting, the complex, the eye-catching. I am always trying to work out what in the room should demand attention and what should not. I want to balance the strong with the subtle, to make sure that when the art is commanding, for example, the mirrors are restrained so the walls do not overwhelm. In this kind of contrast lies harmony, because each component highlights and plays off the other. Think of how much more intense saturated colors become on a rainy day. Or how a bright, sunny day can wash out even the strongest of colors. There really can be too much of a good thing. That principle applies to rooms, also. The eye needs to rest. My challenge lies in working out the most pleasing balance between the pieces that call out, "Look at me!" and those with a quieter presence.

As a teenager, I worked during the summers at Homowack, a resort in the Catskills with the motto Be Nice. During the day, I was a lifeguard. At night, I manned the lights in the nightclub. My first evening on the job, as we were getting the club ready for the show, the manager yelled out at me, "Hey, kid! Pink light, pink light! C'mon, pink light!" I scrambled to find the lights and put them in position. And with the pink lights trained on the stage, the house lights dimmed, the candles on the tables flickering, and the room full of people in their finery, the effect was breathtaking. I also remember what that room looked like when the lights came back up at two a.m. and we still had to clean up. And the next morning, when we were setting it up for the day ahead. Sometimes atmosphere is an illusion. Design's ability to create it is not. Those pink lights taught me a lesson that I have never forgotten about the power of design and decoration to flatter people in a way that heightens not only their appearance, but also their experience. Lighting comes first. And we build from there.

I was reminded of this truth recently in Paris, at a birthday celebration with a client. She commented about how much she loved the atmosphere of the restaurant. As I scanned the room to see what had captivated her, I realized that she was not responding to any individual element, but to the way everything came together. Tea lights on the tables shimmered in the dimness, casting beautiful flickers of candlelight on the surrounding diners, a sort of cool crowd. A buzz filled the room, but it was not noisy. The waiters, who treated us as longtime patrons, added another layer to the experience. On that night, this place was magical for her. But on another night, or at lunchtime, it might not be. You never know. Enchantment lies in that indefinable but very real something in a time and place that you feel but cannot predict.

For my first Kips Bay Decorator Show House in 1995, I was assigned two small maids' rooms, seven feet wide at the most. I decided I was going to design them as a guest suite—a sitting room and a bedroom with a single bed—for myself in another city. One afternoon I left the windows open. It was one of those days in early May when the air felt different. The breeze was soft and scented with spring. The curtains were doing a slow dance with the light. Chet Baker played on the stereo. I noticed a woman poised on the threshold, staring out across the bed and through the window. Finally, she turned to me and said, "I wish I had this room in my house and my children didn't know where it was. I love the atmosphere of this room."

My goal is always to combine the elements of design and decoration to create an environment that makes people comfortable and happy, a mood that they will respond to and remember, an ambience that suits them. If rooms do not look like the people who live in them, those people will never be comfortable in their own skin. Rooms must be about their owners. And expressive of them. Otherwise, the owners look out of place. And if they feel out of place in their home, how then can they make other people feel comfortable?

Atmosphere may be a vague word that means different things to different people. But it is real. We sense it. We create it. We react to it. And we remember it.

OPPOSITE: A seventeenth-century iron Taoist monk, originally used for offerings, sits next to one of Bruno Romeda's sculptures, above a vintage ivory-studded wood box. OVERLEAF, LEFT: This English Regency rosewood console, c. 1805-1810, fits neatly into a niche in the dining room. OVERLEAF, RIGHT: From a big picture point of view, on this wall curves soften straight lines, antique greets modern, and East meets West.

Carefully placed panels of fabric give rhythm and definition to the room's perimeter and softly frame key functional and decorative elements along the walls. Understated patterns in the tablecloth and carpet, my Carrowmore design for Patterson Flynn Martin, play off the scenic wallpaper panels, as do the brass swirls and tendrils of Jacques Jarrige's chandelier. A mask by Robert Courtright centers the objects on the mantel with the gravity of an elemental form.

Deaccessioned from the collection of the Museum of Fine Arts, Boston, and placed on opposite walls, a pair of gilt and polychrome lacquer cabinets dating to the Kangxi period (1662-1772) of the Qing dynasty subtly enhance the dining room's scenic motifs.

PRECEDING PAGES: A Chinese-style lacquer tea table carries the Asian theme into the living room. A Venetian glass shell from the 1950s plays on the table's gilt details. RIGHT: Similar window panels and my "Ogden" carpet for Patterson Flynn Martin tie the living and dining rooms together. Here, though, an understated iron curtain rod provides a line of definition around the upper edge of the space. Pops of blue in different shades and materials add focal points to the soft palette, which helps to make the interior feel full of light. Ample dimensions allow for multiple seating groups and a well-used grand piano that draws focus to the far corner.

CHANGING SCENERY

A few years ago, Jean, my partner, and I started to feel that we wanted to simplify our life in the country. Watching the real estate ads, as I always do, this one-story house built in 1976 caught my eye for several reasons. First, nestled into the trees with the mountains behind, it sat beautifully in the landscape. Second, as a prefabricated "deck house," it belonged to an interesting strand of midcentury design history. (The company that designed and produced it survives today as Acorn Deck House.) Third, it had very good bones, which made for lots of interesting possibilities for a renovation.

Like all the deck houses of its period, this one came with a wood ceiling, exposed joists, and lots of wood paneling. (The owner, an airline pilot well-known and loved in the area, had made it into a bachelor pad with shag carpets, a large bar, a Jacuzzi, and a sauna—all cool in their day, but not for us.) The floor plan was basic, essentially seven rooms and a basement. By the time we added a new garage, pulled down a few walls, and refocused the spaces on the views, the house was the same size, but much more open.

Creating a new front entrance, though, was step one. With the old house, the front door pushed into the living room. Instead, I wanted a contained space—an enclosed transition area to remove coats and boots—that would heighten the surprise of walking into the great room, a living/dining area fronted by a glass wall that opens onto a deck and the vista beyond. To the left of the great room, we put the master

The entry hall of my Connecticut house is a mix of favorite pieces. The painted stone obelisk is a mystery in terms of origin, but to my eye it looks and feels right with the Navajo rug. I had the midcentury Danish credenza lacquered black to fit this space. With the painting by Emilia Dublicki above, the combination fills the eye.

OPPOSITE: A sculptural composition made of car parts dates to the 1960s and animates one wall of the great room. OVERLEAF: The great room decor blends many places and periods. Italian armchairs, c. 1960s, echo the ceiling's angled beams. I purchased the eighteenth-century Irish console for my very first client; when she downsized, she offered it back to me. A stainless-steel box, used as a coffee table, makes a simple backdrop for more interesting objects. Bronka Stern's totem sculpture, c. 1960s, stands tall in one corner.

bedroom, Jean's office, and two baths. To the right, in what used to be the laundry, we installed three doors; one opens to a bar, another to a closet, and a third to the former garage, which I transformed into my home office. I also completely redid the kitchen and reorganized its flow so it had two entrances. To tie all the spaces together further, I used only three colors on the walls: a dark gray-green, and two shades of white, one of which was used for the trim throughout. The rest of the color comes from the furnishings, objects, and artwork.

While the renovation was still underway, someone asked if I were going to do the rooms entirely in midcentury modern or maybe use only pieces from the 1970s. That would have been too obvious a solution. Part of the fun for me was exploring how to use a modern frame to highlight furnishings and objects from other periods and places. My much-edited blend included some pieces I have loved for years, such as a nineteenth-century mirror that first drew me into the world of interiors, and an eighteenth-century Irish console that was the first important piece I purchased for my first client after I had launched my firm, and that she gave to me as a housewarming gift when she decided to downsize. This mix also welcomed others that have more recently caught my eye: an antique Korean chest, a Navajo rug, and a prototype Italian chair from the 1960s. All the pieces have taken on new life in juxtaposition with their fresh surroundings.

This house is about us right now. It is different from our last house, which was about us then. We all evolve.

A nineteenth-century Anglo-Dutch captain's trunk anchors a wall in the entry hall; the dealer stripped and restored its hardware, which a previous owner had painted black. A Robert Courtright mask feels at home in a group of objects that includes a Japanese bronze vase and a Sicilian baroque silvered altar candlestick.

All of my artwork, furnishings, and objects contain stories from my own history. I found this glazed porcelain Nordic god, the top piece off an Austrian stove, in the Portobello Market years ago. The late artists Robert Courtright and Bruno Romeda were a great influence on me and dear friends for more than thirty-five years. The African mask comments on one of Robert's masks elsewhere in the room. Bruno's sculpture literally frames this view.

I created a recessed area for this sofa to ensure that one seating area looks squarely out at the view. The abstract landscape photo above it, one of mine, relates to the scene opposite the sofa. The green pillows help bring hints of the outdoors inside and, like the artwork, introduce moments of saturated color into the neutral environment.

RIGHT: Long and narrow, this room functions as both a dining and a living room with two seating groups. Happily, the ceilings beams divide it neatly into three areas. The Indian stool is a more recent acquisition than many pieces in this space, but an image of something like it had been in my mind's eye for years. OVERLEAF: For privacy, a pocket door separates the entry from the kitchen. The obelisk and a drawing by Pierre Dmitrienko on the wall above it feel naturally connected through form, line, and pattern. In keeping with the overall palette, black and white marble rectangles create a random pattern on the kitchen backsplash. By the door, a collage by Charles Hinman adds a splash of color.

PRECEDING PAGES: Once a garage, my office/guest room is a great place to work, to read, and to daydream while looking at the view. The pillow and bench fabrics energize the space's quiet atmosphere. OPPOSITE: The pattern of the fabric on the bench seems to amplify a similar graphic statement of a vessel by Dana Brandwein, a potter in nearby Sharon, that sits prominently on the low table.

On the opposite side of the room, my desk slips into a wall niche. With a favorite table for books and papers conveniently close by, I have everything I need at my fingertips. The chairs come from a 1940s country club; in their original green patent, they fit right into the interior landscape.

RIGHT: A triptych collage by Robert Courtright draws focus to the wall behind the other seating group in my office/guest room. Used as a side table, a glazed garden stool infuses a bit of shine that contrasts with the pine pedestal. An Indian folding table does similar double duty beside the ebony-finished slat-back chair. OVERLEAF: In Jean's office, a large drawing by James Brown, from the 1980s, fills a recess that seems made for it. We had the top of Jean's French desk, c. 1950, painted red to add a bit of spice into the two-tone palette. An ink drawing by Sewell Sillman hangs above the sofa. On the wall over the desk is a painting by Wayne Cunningham.

There are only three colors on all the interior walls and ceilings, including in our bedroom, where a deer head from Sri Lanka presides from on high. The bed is a prototype of one I designed for Savoir Beds. Gray glass mirrors flank the headboard and reflect back the light and views, which includes the shade of green for the fabric that upholsters the headboard. An antique Korean chest hugs one wall, its hardware introducing a very quiet flourish.

RIGHT: The bedroom opens to its own terrace. A table by the windows holds a number of much-loved objects, including an architectural model of a stage set—perhaps *Tosca* in the round?—found in nearby Hudson, New York. The Bruno Romeda sculpture frames its own perspective.
OVERLEAF: In the master bath, *The Bridge*, a set of four photographs—two on the wall by the sink, the other two above the foot of the tub—shows the restraint and elegance of artist Dorothy Imagire's point of view. It is such a luxury to have a tub that looks directly into the landscape.

PRECEDING PAGES: One of the most appealing aspects of the property is the way the house nests into its surroundings. OPPOSITE: In the summer, the view from the terrace is rich in greens. But when the leaves drop, the mountains dominate. OVERLEAF: Deep in the woods, another corner of the property overlooks the neighbor's horse farm.

TRANSFORMATIONS

The first time I walked into Robert Menhennet's Stone Ridge, New York, house it was the mid-1970s. His antique shop, the Spotted Cow, had really impressed me. But when I saw the rooms he had designed for himself, I was dazzled. They were full of American antiques of different periods, mostly early Federal pieces expertly mixed with some folk art and primitives. My only thought was, "How do I learn about all of this?"

One item in particular, an elaborately carved and gilded nineteenth-century mirror, the first piece of that period I had ever seen outside of a museum, captured my imagination. The more I discovered about it—that it was Regency, from the 1820s, and that its fantastical depictions of a dragon, sea serpents, rocks, and entwined dolphins reflected the period's trend toward exoticism—the more it fixed itself in my mind.

Sadly, Robert's house burned to the ground a few years later. The mirror miraculously survived, although its finish was badly charred. In the restoration, the gilder obscured the carved details. From then on, everyone who looked it saw only what they expected to see—a convex looking glass topped by an eagle—and no more.

I inherited the piece in 1995. since then, despite hanging prominently on a wall, it has been ignored by most (though still loved by me). So I decided to give it a new look as we planned our move. Tanja McGivney, a master gilder, and I developed a silvery tint for overall and a deep verdigris for the creatures. The new finish has made the mirror visible again in a way that captures everyone's attention, just as it did mine the first time I saw it. While several purists have voiced their shock, my feeling is that it is only gilding—and changeable when I pass it on in the distant future!

GIVING BACK

When Anthony Baratta asked me to get involved in the renovation of the Ronald McDonald House of Long Island, it seemed a uniquely rewarding opportunity to use my design skills to give back. The twelve show houses I have done since 1993 were all for wonderful causes. But the Ronald McDonald House spaces would make a difference in people's lives for years to come because its caretaking mission is ongoing: Ronald McDonald House offers to families with hospitalized children a home away from home—with bedrooms, playrooms, and in this case, a New York Mets TV room—that is close to the medical facility.

I grew up a Mets fan, remember the Polo Grounds, and know the team's history from day one. I opted for the Mets TV room, though, because it was an unexpected choice and a great design challenge. Using strip molding to create panel details, a wainscoting of baseball diamonds, and more was a simple way give to the walls architectural definition. The Mets marketing department had lots of team gear, but unfortunately nothing in the way of furnishings. On eBay, I turned up vintage pennants and other memorabilia.

The team's blue and orange palette, so specific, made it hard to find a carpet. After striking out with commercial-grade options and on the Internet, I decided one Saturday afternoon t to try my local carpet store in Connecticut, Laigle Floorcovering and Design. The owner did his best to match my swatches, but no luck. When I finally explained why I needed that particular color combination, he said, "What about the Mets carpet?" I had no clue that one even existed. He pulled out a book of floorcoverings with team logos. And there were the Mets. Home run!

Here come the Amazings! A vintage Mets poster and magazine covers layer moments of happy history into this room, elevating its spirit and giving the children and their families something to smile about. Painting the interiors of the built-in shelving units in the team's shade of glowing orange helps to show off the items on the shelves.

Simple strip molding brings architectural definition to the walls by framing out panels and a baseball diamond-inspired wainscot. Vintage Mets pennants found on eBay flank the sofa by Anthony Lawrence. After searching high, low, and all over the Internet, I thought I had struck out on finding a carpet in colors even close to the Mets blue and orange. Then my local carpet store in Connecticut came to the rescue with this one, a fan's dream and the ultimate piece of team paraphernalia.

ACKNOWLEDGMENTS

First, I would like to thank my clients, who have been so supportive over the years. I am fortunate to decorate only for "nice" people. And I am always grateful for the work.

Sincere thanks to those clients who so graciously allowed us into their homes to photograph them for this book.

My team has worked hard on behalf of this book and all our projects. Many thanks to Rachel Webster, Bobbi Chadwell, Nick Cohen, and Margaret Barrett for all their help.

I always consider myself lucky to have met my agent Jill Cohen. She is always positive, practical and encouraging. Many thanks also to Doug Turshen for his exacting eye and inspired art direction and to Judith Nasatir, who always makes my rambling words complete, interesting and fun to read.

Sincere appreciation to The Monacelli Press and editor Elizabeth White for taking on another book project with me and making it all happen.

Wendy Goodman is the most wonderful friend and a legend in the design industry. She has been a generous promoter of my work over the years. I am so grateful and touched that she agreed to write the foreword.

Simon Upton, John Gruen, and Pieter Estersohn, the wonderful photographers whose images make my work look good, thank you for your talent and vision. The amazing Mieke ten Have and Howard Christian both worked magic and were delightful to be with. Raina Kattelson and Anna Molvik each brought their unique style to the locations.

I am especially grateful to all the publishers, editors and writers who have been kind enough to feature my work over the years. Thank you, Marion McEvoy, Margaret Russell, Michael Boodro and Whitney Robinson. Thanks also to Ingrid Abramovitch, Parker Larson, Karen Marks and Charles Curkin. Special thanks to Alison Levasseur, who has always been gracious, and to the gifted writers Mitch Owens and Suzanne Slesin, who included me in many articles early in my career. I am also very grateful to D.J. Carey, Kendall Cronstrom, Marianne Howaston, Ann Maine, Jill Wagge, Jane Garmey, Jason Kontos, Stacey Bewkes, Cindy Allen, Robert Ruffino, Clint Smith, and Steele Marcoux, as well as Alanna Gallagher of The Irish Times.

Working with many great architects over the years has been an honor. I have been especially fortunate to have had multiple projects with Peter Pennoyer, Jim Joseph, Douglas Vanderhorn and Charlotte Worthy, each of whom is generous, thoughtful, and the ultimate professional.

I so appreciate every opportunity to collaborate with wonderful craftspeople, workrooms and dealers. Sincere thanks to Danny Murphy, Kevin Campbell, Ciara Farrell, Peter Caffrey, Chris Cozzarin, Jonas Upholstery, Anthony Lawrence/ Belfair, Interior Haberdashery, Alan Schatzberg, Janus et Cie, Florian Papp, David Duncan, BK Antiques, Balsamo, Valerie Goodman, Patricia Grey, Apter-Fredricks and Alphonse Sutter.

I am very grateful to Gerald and Stephen Puschel of F. Schumacher and PFM, who have been so generous and supportive. I am proud of my fabric, wallpaper and carpet collections and thank Dara Caponigro for promoting them so beautifully.

People I truly respect and admire have encouraged my own photography from early on with kind words and sage advice. Sincere thanks to Margaret Russell, Marion McEvoy, Lisa and Jeff Bewkes, Stephen Farrington, Elaine Griffen, Becky Birdwell and Annie Kelly. I will also be forever grateful for the inspiration I receive from the true pros, the photographers Gerald Incandela, Peter Margonelli, Fredrick-Edwin Bertin, Tim Street-Porter and Anne Day.

No words can adequately express how much I appreciate my close circle of friends, who support me on a daily basis: Alexis Contant, Liv Ballard, Anne Day, Deborah Rathburn, Dennis Lee, Janice Langrall, Rob Burden, Patrick Gallagher, Beatrice Philippe, Inge Heckel, Tony Korner, Jane Schott, Maria Kelsey, Jamie Lehrer, Teresa Hothem, Jeff Brody, Mona Levine, Dan Dwyer, Natasha Bergreen, and Mindy Papp.

I am grateful to my new Instagram friends who encourage me to post, especially Karen Ingram, Suzanne Williams, and Barbara Beresford.

Carol and Richard Kalikow, thank you for moving to Salisbury and letting me follow you there. I am grateful for all of your kind introductions, which have made a big difference in my life and career.

I am forever indebted to David Easton for the invaluable training and experience.

Thank you to my sisters, brother, nephews, niece, cousins, and my aunts, Eileen Kent and Catherine Ruquet, for all your support.

PHOTOGRAPHY CREDITS

Pieter Estersohn: 123–25, 127–31, 133–40, 142
Styling by Howard Christian

John Gruen: 10, 19, 22, 23, 25, 53, 56, 57, 61–64, 67, 69–72, 73, 75–78, 80–83, 85–87, 89–91, 93, 94, 96–99,101,105, 109–11, 113–17, 119–21, 147, 150–58, 159–62, 164,165, 167–69, 171, 173 175, 177, 179–82, 184, 186, 187, 189, 190, 195, 199, 200–203, 205–209, 250, 252
Styling by Mieke ten Have: projects on pages 68–101, 174–191
Styling by Anna Molvik: project on pages 104–121
Styling by Raina Kattleson: projects on pages 146–163, 194–208

Simon Upton: Cover, 2, 6,15, 27, 29, 30, 32, 34–38, 40–43, 45–47, 49, 211, 213–15, 217–19, 221–26, 228 ,229, 231–39, 241–43, 245–47, 249
Styling by Mieke ten Have

Julian Schnabel, *Maria Callas #2P,* (p. 164): © 2020 Julian Schnabel/Artists Rights Society (ARS) New York

ENDPAPER: Gabrielle Embroidery, one of my designs for F. Schumacher & Co.
PAGE 2: Great room of my Connecticut house.
PAGE 6: A silkscreen by Jennifer Bartlett above an early American vinegar-painted trunk in my Connecticut entry hall.

First published in the United States by The Monacelli Press. All rights reserved.

Library of Congress Control Number: 2020935626

ISBN: 9781580935418

Design: Doug Turshen and Steve Turner

Printed in China

The Monacelli Press
65 Bleecker Street
New York, New York 10012